XTREME ROBOTS

Humanoid Robots

S.L. HAMILTON

A&D Xtreme
An imprint of Abdo Publishing | abdobooks.com

abdobooks.com

Published by Abdo Publishing, a division of ABDO,
PO Box 398166, Minneapolis, Minnesota 55439.
Copyright ©2019 by Abdo Consulting Group, Inc.
International copyrights reserved in all countries.
No part of this book may be reproduced in any form
without written permission from the publisher. A&D
Xtreme™ is a trademark and logo of Abdo Publishing.

Printed in the United States of America, North Mankato, MN.
112018
012019

Editor: John Hamilton
Copy Editor: Bridget O'Brien
Graphic Design: Sue Hamilton
Cover Design: Candice Keimig and Pakou Moua
Cover Photo: NASA
Interior Photos & Illustrations: Alvark Tokyo-pg 27 (bottom inset);
American Honda Motor Co.-pgs 6 & 7 (middle left); AP-pgs 7 (top left
& bottom), 21 (bottom), 26 & 27 (bottom); Boston Dynamics-pgs 8 & 9;
DARPA-pg 21 (middle); DLR-pg 19; Frederic Osada & Teddy Seguin/
DRASSM-pgs 14 & 15; FUJISOFT-pg 18; Instituto Italiano di Technologia-
pgs 12 & 13; iStock-pgs 2-3; JAXA-pg 24; KAIST-pgs 1 & 20; KYODO-pg
18 (inset); NASA-pgs 4-5, 22, 23, 25 & 30-31; Shutterstock-pgs 7 (top
right), 16, 17, 28, 29 & 32; Tosy-pg 27 (top); U.S. Navy-pgs 10 & 11;
University of Nevada, Las Vegas-pg 21 (top).

Library of Congress Control Number: 2018950010
Publisher's Cataloging-in-Publication Data

Names: Hamilton, S.L., author.
Title: Humanoid robots / by S.L. Hamilton.
Description: Minneapolis, Minnesota : Abdo Publishing, 2019 |
Series: Xtreme robots | Includes online resources and index.
Identifiers: ISBN 9781532118258 (lib. bdg.) |
ISBN 9781532171437 (ebook)
Subjects: LCSH: Humanoid robots--Juvenile literature.
| Artificial intelligence--Juvenile literature. |
Androids--Juvenile literature. |
Robots--Juvenile literature.
Classification: DDC 629.892--dc23

Contents

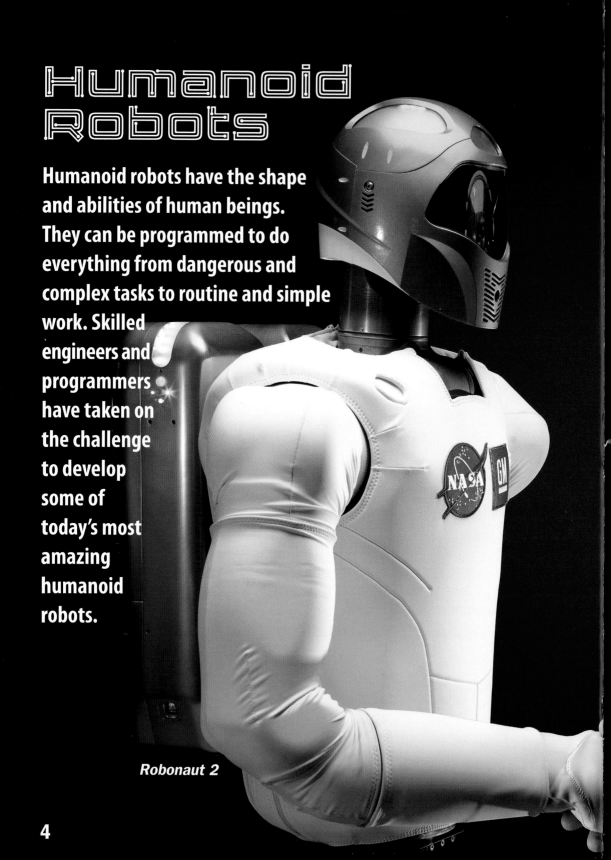

Humanoid Robots

Humanoid robots have the shape and abilities of human beings. They can be programmed to do everything from dangerous and complex tasks to routine and simple work. Skilled engineers and programmers have taken on the challenge to develop some of today's most amazing humanoid robots.

Robonaut 2

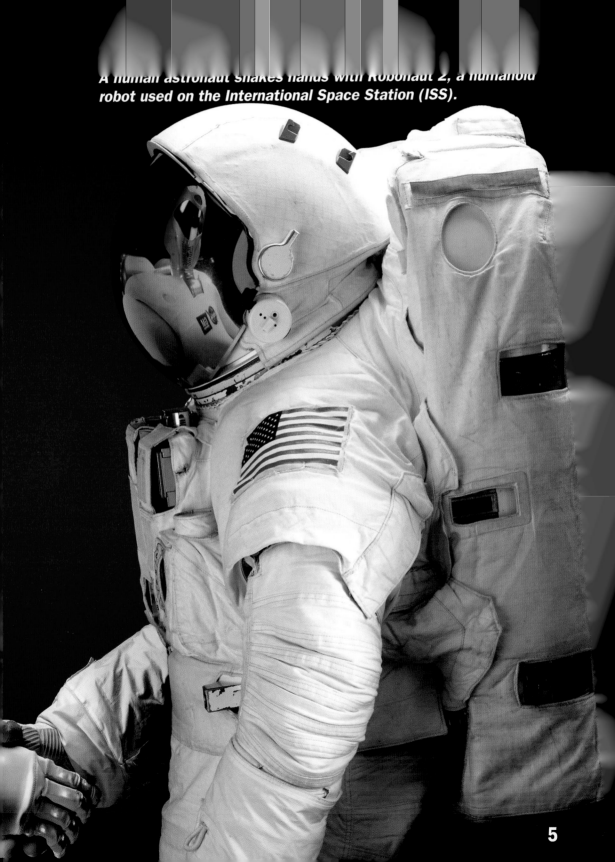

A human astronaut shakes hands with Robonaut 2, a humanoid robot used on the International Space Station (ISS).

Early Humanoid Robots

Honda Motor Company began developing a walking robot in 1986. Walking is very difficult for robots. Humans balance and adjust their steps without really thinking about it. But for robots, every tiny adjustment needs to be thought of and programmed. Honda's engineers began with just legs. They went through many stages. In 2000, ASIMO (Advanced Step in Innovative MObility) was introduced to the world. This cute humanoid robot could walk, run, climb stairs, grasp objects, and even recognize faces and respond to voice commands. It showed the world what robots could do.

XTREME FACT – *A robot that can walk on two legs is called a bipedal robot.*

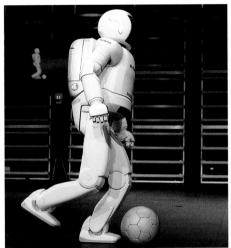

ASIMO is 4 feet 3 inches (1.3 m) tall and weighs 110 pounds (50 kg).

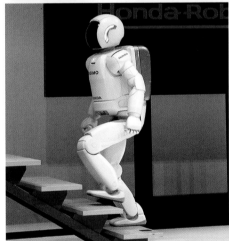

ASIMO has been programmed to run on uneven ground, climb stairs, grasp trays, and even conduct an orchestra!

Search & Rescue Humanoid Robots

Humanoid robots can help first responders in search and rescue (SAR). They can go where it's too dangerous for people. Boston Dynamics' Atlas is about 5 feet (1.5 m) tall and weighs 165 pounds (75 kg). This big, sturdy humanoid robot can move its arms and legs, and bend at the waist. It can walk and run. Atlas's many sensors allow it to move across uneven or rough ground. It can even pick itself up if it falls over. As a SAR assistant, it can move or carry heavy objects, clearing the way to reach people in trouble.

Boston Dynamics

Atlas

Atlas has amazing abilities. It can run across rough ground. The humanoid robot has even been programmed to do a backflip!

SAFFir (Shipboard Autonomous Firefighting Robot) is being tested by the United States Navy. SAFFir (pronounced "safer") is 5 feet 10 inches (1.8 m) tall and weighs 140 pounds (63.5 kg). It has thermal imaging that lets it locate a fire behind a door on a ship. The sensors also allow it to avoid victims that could be in the area. Once near the fire, SAFFir uses its powerful gripper "hands" to hold a fire hose and put out the flames.

SAFFir

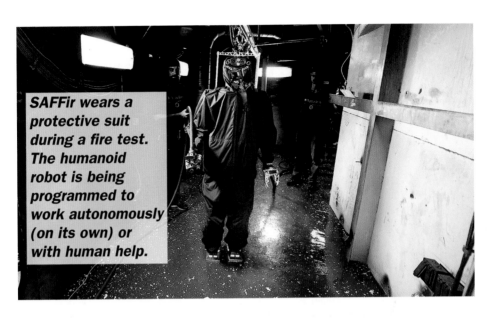

SAFFir wears a protective suit during a fire test. The humanoid robot is being programmed to work autonomously (on its own) or with human help.

SAFFir puts out a shipboard fire with researcher assistance. The robot may help protect sailors from smoke and fire dangers.

XTREME QUOTE – "We're working toward human-robot teams. It's what we call the hybrid force: humans and robots working together." –Dr. Thomas McKenna, Office of Naval Research

WALK-MAN is a disaster-response robot. It is built in Italy by the Instituto Italiano di Technologia. It is 6 feet (1.85 m) tall and weighs 225 pounds (102 kg). The jointed robot can walk and balance by itself, but a human operator controls WALK-MAN through many of its tasks. It can lift and move rubble. Its arms can hold up to 22 pounds (10 kg). The long fingers are able to reach out to grasp and turn door handles or operate tools. WALK-MAN can work in dangerous areas with a battery life of up to 2 hours.

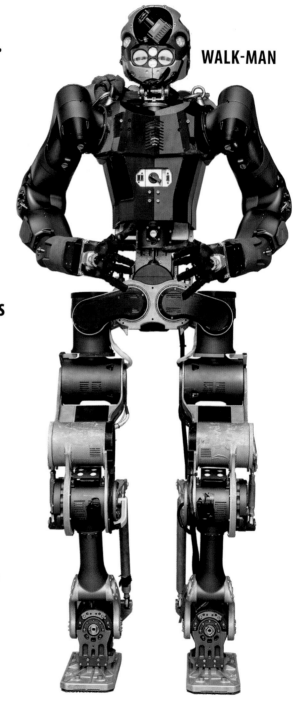

WALK-MAN

WALK-MAN moves rubble.

WALK-MAN opens a door.

WALK-MAN uses a fire extinguisher.

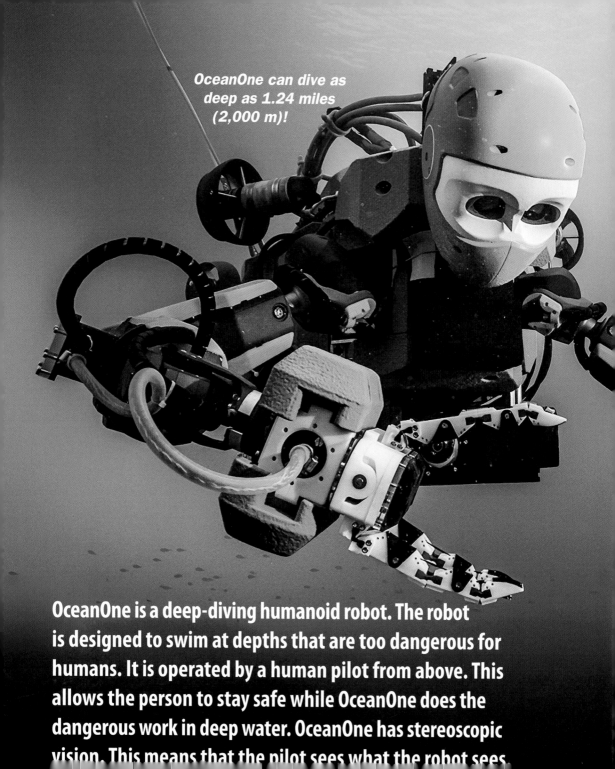

OceanOne can dive as deep as 1.24 miles (2,000 m)!

OceanOne is a deep-diving humanoid robot. The robot is designed to swim at depths that are too dangerous for humans. It is operated by a human pilot from above. This allows the person to stay safe while OceanOne does the dangerous work in deep water. OceanOne has stereoscopic vision. This means that the pilot sees what the robot sees.

OceanOne and pilot discover a vase from the La Lune, a ship that went down in 1664.

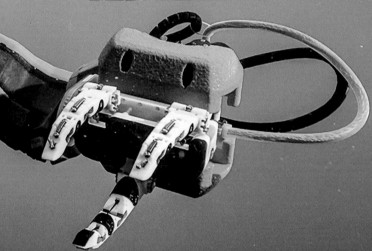

OceanOne is 5 feet (1.5 m) long. It has 8 thrusters that move it through the water. In 2016, OceanOne explored a shipwreck in the Mediterranean Sea. It dove to a depth of 328 feet (100 m). Each of OceanOne's hands has force sensors that let the human pilot "feel" what OceanOne feels. The human/robot team safely collected artifacts from the seafloor. OceanOne proved its abilities in deepwater archaeology, but it may one day be used in search and rescue, mining, and other high-risk tasks.

Service Humanoid Robots

Pepper

Robots that perform tasks useful to the well-being of humans are called service robots. They work autonomously (on their own) or with human help. These robots may do anything from household chores to giving directions. Pepper is the first humanoid robot able to recognize people's faces and basic human emotions. Created by SoftBank Robotics, Pepper is 4 feet (1.2 m) tall. This sweet-faced robot can speak 15 languages and answer questions using either its voice or its touchpad screen.

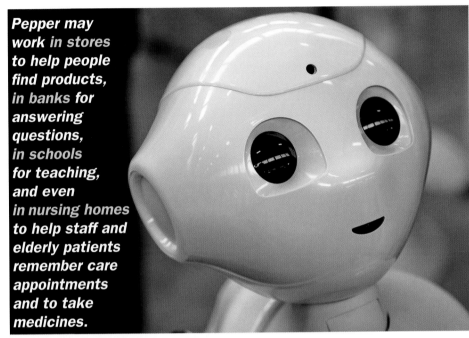

Pepper may work in stores to help people find products, in banks for answering questions, in schools for teaching, and even in nursing homes to help staff and elderly patients remember care appointments and to take medicines.

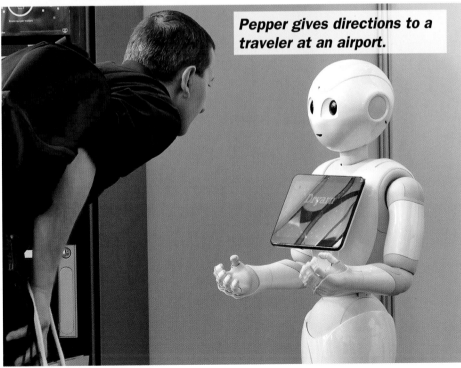

Pepper gives directions to a traveler at an airport.

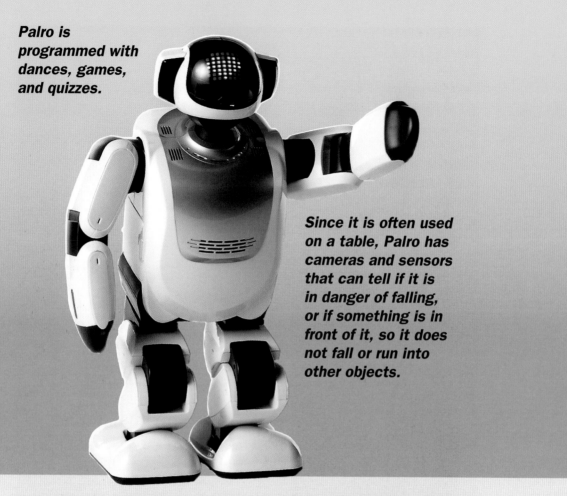

Palro is programmed with dances, games, and quizzes.

Since it is often used on a table, Palro has cameras and sensors that can tell if it is in danger of falling, or if something is in front of it, so it does not fall or run into other objects.

Palro (pal + robot) is a health-services humanoid robot. Created by FUJISOFT, it is used in places where there are not enough caregivers. The 15.75-inch (40-cm) -tall robot is a helpful assistant. Palro can answer questions, respond to verbal commands, recognize faces and voices, and even lead exercise routines.

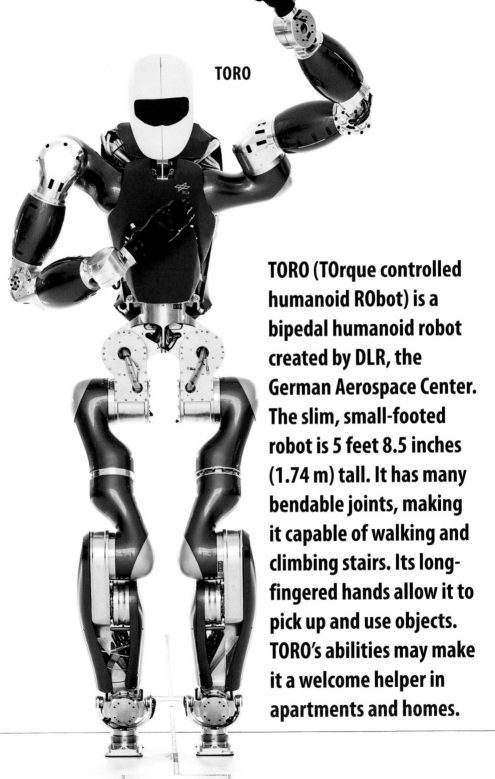

TORO

TORO (TOrque controlled humanoid RObot) is a bipedal humanoid robot created by DLR, the German Aerospace Center. The slim, small-footed robot is 5 feet 8.5 inches (1.74 m) tall. It has many bendable joints, making it capable of walking and climbing stairs. Its long-fingered hands allow it to pick up and use objects. TORO's abilities may make it a welcome helper in apartments and homes.

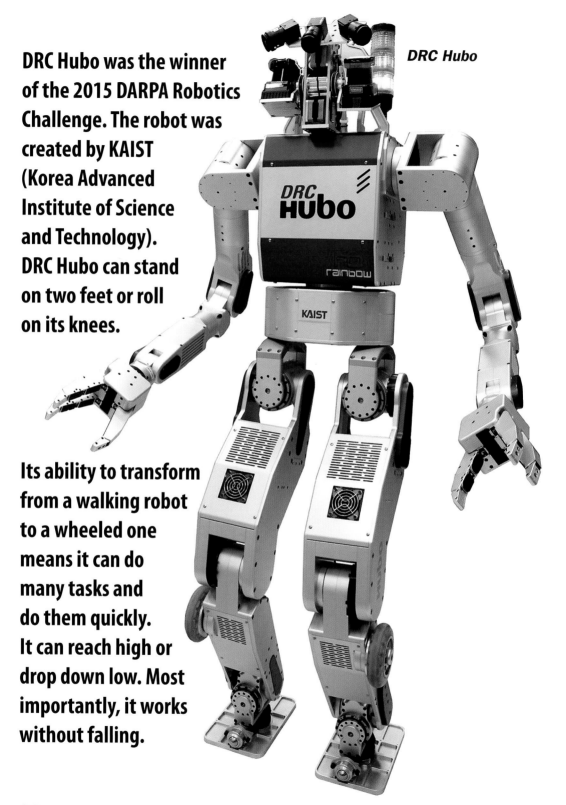

DRC Hubo was the winner of the 2015 DARPA Robotics Challenge. The robot was created by KAIST (Korea Advanced Institute of Science and Technology). DRC Hubo can stand on two feet or roll on its knees.

Its ability to transform from a walking robot to a wheeled one means it can do many tasks and do them quickly. It can reach high or drop down low. Most importantly, it works without falling.

DRC Hubo

DRC Hubo drives a car during the 2015 DARPA Robotics Challenge. Getting out of the car was also one of its tasks. DRC Hubo succeeded at this, too.

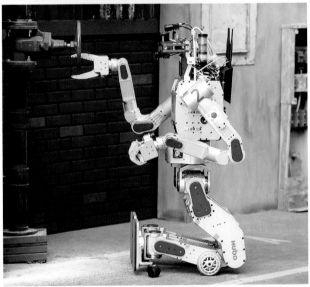

DRC Hubo's lower legs have wheels on the knees and casters on the feet. This gives the robot great flexibility. Here it has located and successfully closed a valve during the 2015 DARPA Robotics Challenge.

DRC Hubo carries an Olympic torch during the Olympic Torch Relay in South Korea on December 11, 2017. The 2018 Winter Olympic Games were held in Pyeongchang, South Korea.

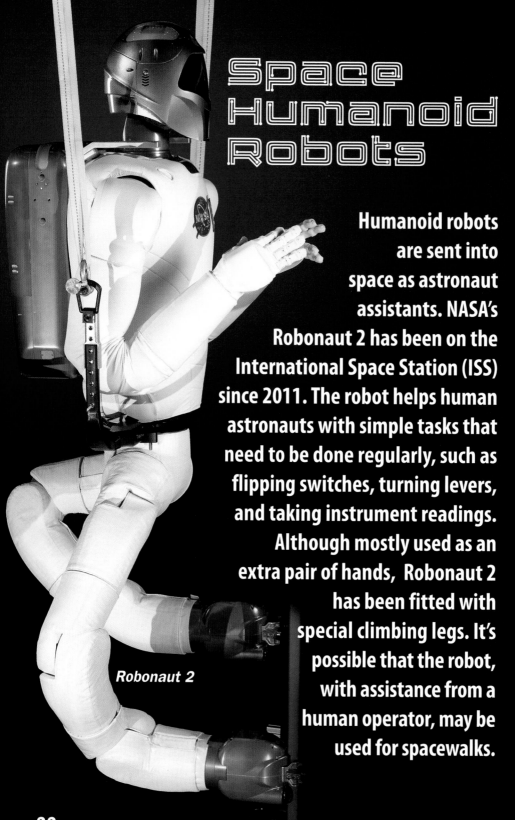

Space Humanoid Robots

Humanoid robots are sent into space as astronaut assistants. NASA's Robonaut 2 has been on the International Space Station (ISS) since 2011. The robot helps human astronauts with simple tasks that need to be done regularly, such as flipping switches, turning levers, and taking instrument readings. Although mostly used as an extra pair of hands, Robonaut 2 has been fitted with special climbing legs. It's possible that the robot, with assistance from a human operator, may be used for spacewalks.

Robonaut 2

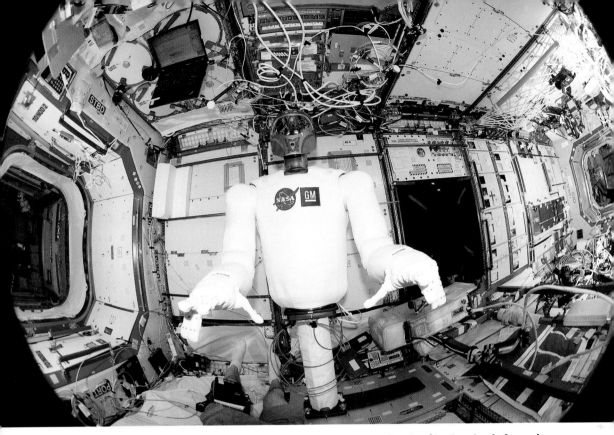

Robonaut 2 works with an astronaut on dexterity tests (above) and a systems check (below) on the International Space Station.

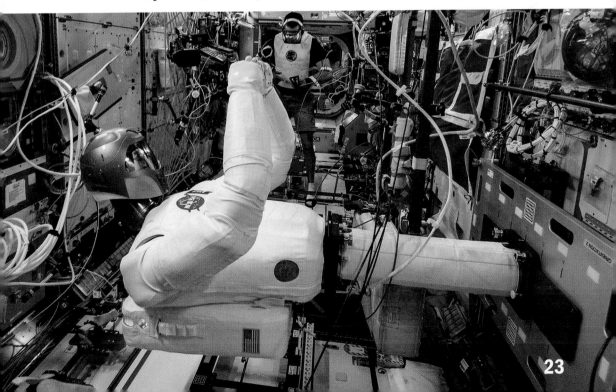

Kirobo

Kirobo is a mini-humanoid robot that stands 13 inches (34 cm) tall. It was sent to the ISS in 2013 by JAXA (Japan Aerospace Exploration Agency). Kirobo's mission was to test human-robot interaction in space. Kirobo can recognize human voices, faces, and emotions. It can carry on conversations with astronauts. Having a robot to talk to may help astronauts on long voyages.

The first conversation in space between a robot and a human was in Japanese. Kirobo talked with astronaut Koichi Wakata aboard the ISS on Friday, December 6, 2013.

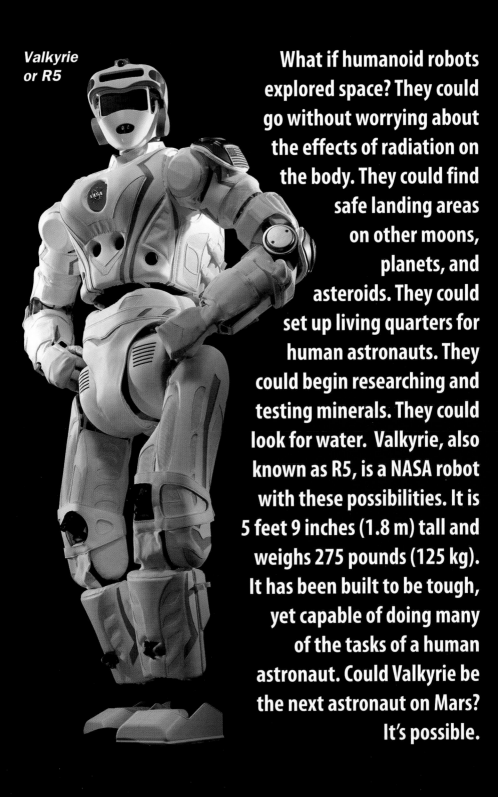

Valkyrie or R5

What if humanoid robots explored space? They could go without worrying about the effects of radiation on the body. They could find safe landing areas on other moons, planets, and asteroids. They could set up living quarters for human astronauts. They could begin researching and testing minerals. They could look for water. Valkyrie, also known as R5, is a NASA robot with these possibilities. It is 5 feet 9 inches (1.8 m) tall and weighs 275 pounds (125 kg). It has been built to be tough, yet capable of doing many of the tasks of a human astronaut. Could Valkyrie be the next astronaut on Mars? It's possible.

Sports Humanoid Robots

Programming and engineering come together to create humanoid robot athletes who compete in a variety of sports. SoftBank Robotics' NAO (pronounced "now") robots are 23 inches (58 cm) tall. They are competitors in the RoboCup soccer league. The robots are fully autonomous. When a game is being played, the only human who participates is the referee.

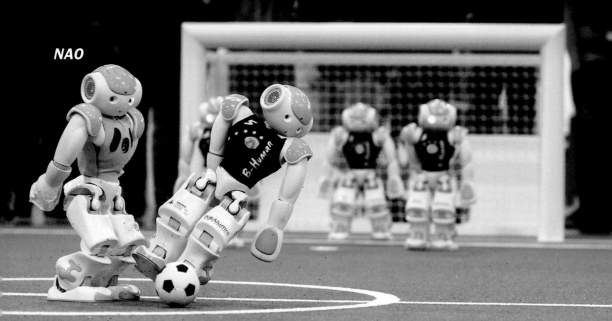

NAO robot teams Berlin United (blue vest) and team B-Human (black vests) compete in the German RoboCup Junior Championship. The winning team goes on to represent Germany in the world championship RoboCup, held each year in various countries.

NAO

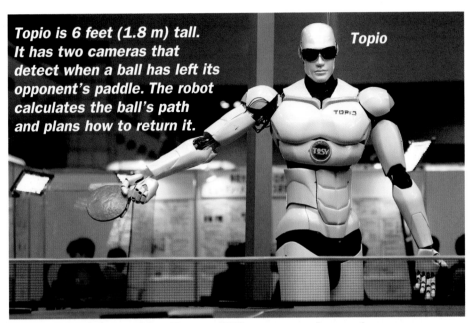

Topio is 6 feet (1.8 m) tall. It has two cameras that detect when a ball has left its opponent's paddle. The robot calculates the ball's path and plans how to return it.

Topio

Topio, developed by Tosy of Vietnam, plays ping-pong against a human player. CUE is a free-throw expert built by Toyota. The basketball-shooting robot has 100% accuracy.

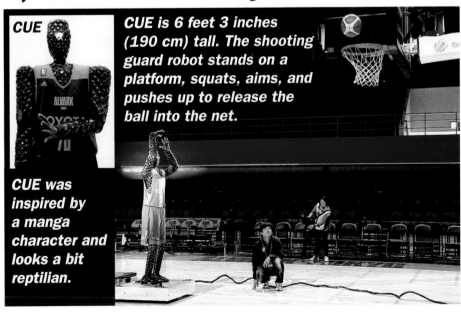

CUE

CUE is 6 feet 3 inches (190 cm) tall. The shooting guard robot stands on a platform, squats, aims, and pushes up to release the ball into the net.

CUE was inspired by a manga character and looks a bit reptilian.

AI Humanoid Robots

Could robots learn and think for themselves? Artificial intelligence (AI) is the next step for humanoid robots. Sophia is an AI robot developed by Hanson Robotics. The robot has the ability to listen and respond to certain words and phrases, along with matching facial expressions. Sometimes called "machine intelligence," this programming is still in the early stages. People question if robots with AI will be a good or bad thing.

Sophia

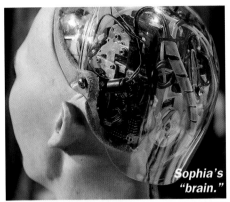

Sophia's "brain."

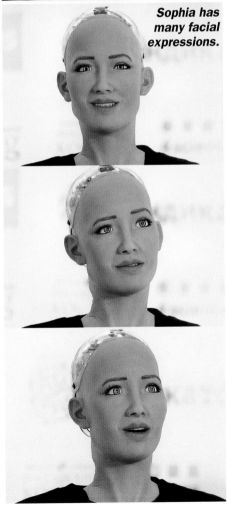

Sophia has many facial expressions.

A full-length view of Sophia. The robot stands on a rolling platform.

Glossary

ARCHAEOLOGY
A scientific area where people search for, uncover, and study artifacts from the past in order to learn how people of ancient societies once lived.

AUTONOMOUS
Able to work on its own. An autonomous robot does not have a human operating it.

DARPA
The Defense Advanced Research Projects Agency is part of the United States Department of Defense. The agency's need to keep people safe in dangerous and toxic environments has led DARPA to host robotic challenges that result in awards of prize money for winning robot design teams.

DEXTERITY
The ability to do various tasks, usually with the hands.

ENGINEER
A person whose job is to use scientific knowledge to create and maintain mechanical and electronic objects and structures. This includes such things as robots, cameras, and engines.

First Responders

People such as police, firefighters, ambulance drivers, emergency medical technicians (EMTs), and paramedics, who are the first on the scene of an emergency situation.

Humanoid

Something that looks like a human.

Joints

Areas of a body where two parts are linked together. Joints include neck, shoulder, elbow, wrist, finger, knee, hip, ankle, foot, and more. Joints let parts of the robot bend, twist, rotate, and turn.

Manga

A style of Japanese comic books and graphic novels.

Sensors

In robots, devices that send out signals and get information from a surrounding area. The robot's computers may use the data to decide what the robot should do next, or pass the collected information on to a human operator.

Online Resources

Booklinks
NONFICTION NETWORK
FREE! ONLINE NONFICTION RESOURCES

To learn more about humanoid robots, visit abdobooklinks.com. These links are routinely monitored and updated to provide the most current information available.

index